Colombia

by Tracey Boraas

Content Consultant:
Maurice P. Brungardt, Professor of Latin American History
Loyola University
New Orleans, Louisiana

Reading Consultant:
Dr. Robert Miller, Professor of Special Education
Minnesota State University, Mankato

Bridgestone Books
an imprint of Capstone Press
Mankato, Minnesota

Bridgestone Books are published by Capstone Press
151 Good Counsel Drive, P.O. Box 669, Mankato, Minnesota 56002
http://www.capstone-press.com

Library of Congress Cataloging-in-Publication Data
Boraas, Tracey.
    Colombia/by Tracey Boraas; content consultant, Maurice P. Brungardt.
    p. cm.—(Countries and cultures)
    Includes bibliographical references and index.
    Summary: An introduction to the geography, history, economy, culture,
and people of Colombia.
    ISBN 0-7368-1076-5
    1. Colombia—Juvenile literature. [1. Colombia.] I. Title. II. Series.
F2258.5 .B67 2002
986.1—dc21   2001005130

Editorial Credits
Gillia M. Olson, editor; Heather Kindseth, cover designer and interior layout
    designer; Heidi Meyer, interior illustrator; Alta Schaffer, photo researcher

Photo Credits
AFP/CORBIS, 29, 32; Bauer/Bruce Coleman, Inc., 19; Bettmann/CORBIS, 20,
27; Betty Crowell, 55; Capstone Press/Gary Sundermeyer, 51; Chip & Rosa
Maria Peterson, 34, 46, 49; Dave G. Houser/Houserstock, 8, 45; DigitalVision,
13; Flat Earth Collection, 1 (all), 15, 31, 42; Frank Lane Picture
Agency/CORBIS, 56; Greg Johnston, cover (right); North Wind Picture
Archives, 22, 25; One Mile Up, Inc., 57 (both); PhotoDisc, Inc., cover (left);
Provided by: Audrius Tomonis-www.banknotes.com, 41(bills); Victor Englebert,
4, 12, 17, 39, 53, 63

Artistic Effects
Capstone Press; Flat Earth Collection; PhotoDisc, Inc.

1 2 3 4 5 6 07 06 05 04 03 02

Contents

Chapter 1
Fast Facts about Colombia 4
Explore Colombia 5
Chapter 2
Fast Facts about Colombia's Land 8
The Land, Climate, and Wildlife 9
Chapter 3
Fast Facts about Colombia's History 20
Colombia's History and Government 21
Chapter 4
Fast Facts about Colombia's Economy 34
Colombia's Economy 35
Chapter 5
Fast Facts about Colombia's People 42
People, Culture, and Daily Life 43

Maps
Geopolitical Map of Colombia 7
Colombia's Land Regions and Topography 10
Colombia's Industries and Natural Resources 36

Features
Jaguars 19
Colombia's Money 41
Learn to Speak Spanish 49
Recipe: Make Fried Plantains 51
Colombia's National Symbols 57
Timeline 58
Words to Know 60
To Learn More 61
Useful Addresses 62
Internet Sites 62
Index 64

Fast Facts about Colombia

Official name: Republic of Colombia

Location: Northern South America

Bordering countries and waters: Brazil, Ecuador, Panama, Peru, Venezuela, Caribbean Sea, Pacific Ocean

National population: 40,349,388

Capital city: Santafé de Bogotá

Major cities and populations: Santafé de Bogotá (6,288,000), Medellín (2,951,000), Cali (2,710,000), Barranquilla (1,736,000), Cartagena (812,595)

Explore Colombia

The Andes Mountains in Colombia are alive with volcanic activity. The Puracé Volcano in Puracé Volcano National Park stands 15,604 feet (4,756 meters) high. Visitors to the park witness amazing signs of volcanic activity, including hot springs; flowing rivers of milky, sulfurous water; and steaming vents in Earth's surface.

The Galeras Volcano, near the small city of Pasto in southwestern Colombia, is an active volcano high in the Andes. In 1993, Galeras erupted, killing nine scientists who were studying the volcano.

Nevado del Ruiz, west of Santafé de Bogotá, is the world's fourth deadliest volcano. In 1985, capped with an enormous amount of ice and snow, it stood 17,453 feet (5,320 meters) high. An eruption on November 13, 1985, melted a small part of the ice cap. The melting ice water mixed with volcanic ash and dirt. The resulting mudflow, called a lahar, raced down the

◀ Puracé Volcano's eruption left behind a large depression at its peak.

mountain's steep slopes and buried the city of Armero. In total, 23,000 people died.

Colombia

Snow-topped volcanoes are only a sample of Colombia's varied landscape. Beaches, deserts, and forests also cover the country.

Colombia is located on the northwestern corner of South America, with coastlines on the Caribbean Sea and Pacific Ocean. Colombia's border on the Isthmus of Panama is the only land route between North and South America. Colombia also shares a border with Venezuela and Brazil to the east and Peru and Ecuador to the south.

Colombia is the fourth largest country in South America, covering 439,733 square miles (1,138,910 square kilometers). It is about four times the size of the U.S. state of Nevada. Colombia has a population of about 40 million.

Colombia is a developing country with one of the healthiest economies in South America, although it remains politically troubled. Violence resulting from the illegal drug trade and rebel political groups threatens the safety of Colombians and tourists. Colombia's government is working to stop the drug trade and to promote peace with different rebel groups.

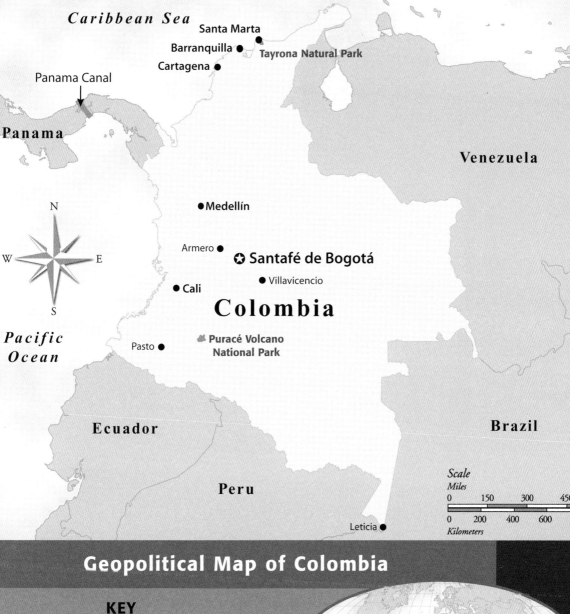

Caribbean Sea

Santa Marta

Barranquilla ●

Tayrona Natural Park

Cartagena ●

Panama Canal

Panama

Venezuela

N

W — E

S

●Medellín

Armero ●

✪ **Santafé de Bogotá**

● Villavicencio

● Cali

Colombia

Pacific Ocean

🌋 **Puracé Volcano National Park**

Pasto ●

Ecuador

Brazil

Peru

Leticia ●

Scale
Miles
0   150   300   450

0   200   400   600   800
Kilometers

Geopolitical Map of Colombia

KEY

✪ CAPITAL

● CITIES

National Parks

Fast Facts about Colombia's Land

Area: 439,733 square miles (1,138,910 square kilometers)

Latitude and longitude of geographic center: 4 degrees north latitude, 72 degrees west longitude

Highest elevation: Cristóbal Colón, 18,947 feet (5,775 meters)

Lowest elevation: Pacific Ocean, sea level

Chapter 2

The Land, Climate, and Wildlife

Colombia's varied landscape is divided into five main geographical regions. These are the Caribbean Coast, the Pacific Lowlands, the Andes Mountains, the Eastern Plains, and the Amazon Rain Forest. Colombia's location near the equator gives it a tropical climate. But temperatures do change with elevation.

The Caribbean Coast

The Caribbean Coast region stretches along the northern border of Colombia. Colombia's 1,000 miles (1,600 kilometers) of Caribbean Sea coastline boasts white sandy beaches, palm trees, and clear, sparkling water. Islands such as San Andrés and Old Providence are located about 480 miles (772 kilometers) northwest of the Colombian mainland.

The Caribbean Coast region contains people, industry, historic areas, and natural parks. Nearly

◀ The Spanish built this fortress that overlooks Cartagena's Caribbean coast.

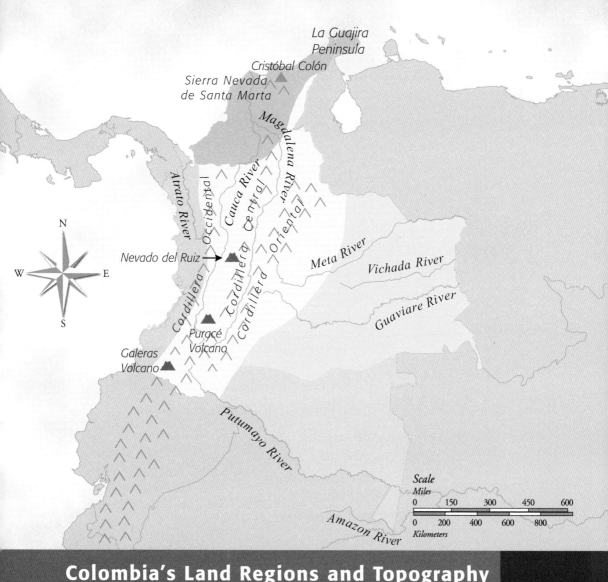

La Guajira
Peninsula
Cristóbal Colón
Sierra Nevada
de Santa Marta
Magdalena River
Atrato River
Occidental
Cauca River
Central
Cordillera
Oriental
Nevado del Ruiz →
Cordillera
Cordillera
Meta River
Vichada River
Guaviare River
Puracé
Volcano
Galeras
Volcano
Putumayo River
Amazon River

Scale
Miles
0   150   300   450   600
0   200   400   600   800
Kilometers

N
W   E
S

Colombia's Land Regions and Topography

KEY

- Caribbean Coast
- Pacific Lowlands
- Andes Mountains
- Eastern Plains
- Amazon Rain Forest
- Rivers

- ▲ Volcanoes
- △ Mountain
- ∧ Mountain Ranges

20 percent of Colombia's people live there. The port cities of Barranquilla, Cartagena, and Santa Marta lie on the coast. These cities contain most of the region's industry. East of Santa Marta, the Tayrona Natural Park covers 37,000 acres (14,974 hectares). Green turtles nest in the park's beaches.

The Sierra Nevada de Santa Marta mountain range lies in the Caribbean Coast region. This isolated mountain range includes Colombia's highest point, Cristóbal Colón, which rises 18,947 feet (5,775 meters). Animals such as anteaters, sloths, and armadillos make their homes in the forests of the mountains.

Most of the Caribbean coast has daily rainfall, averaging 40 to 70 inches (102 to 178 centimeters) of rain each year. But the region also contains Colombia's driest area, Guajira Peninsula. It receives a yearly rainfall of less than 30 inches (76 centimeters). This peninsula extends from Colombia's northern tip to the Caribbean Sea. Lizards, snakes, huge tortoises, and armadillos live in this dry area.

Pacific Lowlands

The swampy, thickly forested Pacific Lowlands region lies along the Pacific Ocean. At sea level, this region is Colombia's lowest point. The southern Pacific coast receives the same average rainfall as the Caribbean

▼ Mangrove trees form root clusters in swamps along Colombia's Pacific coast.

Coast region. The Chocó, one of the wettest places in the world, is a 550-mile (885-kilometer) stretch of tropical mangrove swamp along the Pacific coast and the Atrato River. The Chocó receives heavy rains almost every day, with an average annual rainfall of more than 420 inches (1,067 centimeters).

The tropical rain forest and warm ocean waters combine to form a rich natural environment for plants and animals. More than 450 of Colombia's 1,800 bird species live within the Chocó. Monkeys, raccoons, deer, and piglike peccaries make their homes in the Chocó. Large rodents such as agoutis, pacas, and capybaras inhabit the forest and swampy areas. Wild cats such as pumas and jaguars prowl these forests, while crocodiles and gentle manatees swim in the Chocó's swamps.

Chocó, or poison-arrow, frog

The Andes Mountains

The Andes Mountains tower over one-third of Colombia. The Andes are divided into three cordilleras, or mountain ranges, that run parallel to the Pacific Ocean coast. The Cordillera Occidental is closest to the Pacific coast, followed by the Cordillera Central and Cordillera Oriental.

Lush valleys lie between the ranges. The Cauca River separates the Cordillera Occidental and the Cordillera Central ranges. As it flows to the Caribbean Sea, the Magdalena River divides the Cordillera Central and the Cordillera Oriental ranges. Broad-leaved evergreen trees are thought to have once covered the valleys and all but the highest slopes of the Andes. But people have cleared much of the land for farming and mining.

About 75 percent of Colombia's people live in the Andes. Santafé de Bogotá, usually shortened to Bogotá, is located on a plateau about 8,660 feet (2,640 meters) high. Bogotá is Colombia's capital and largest city.

Colombia's coolest temperatures are found in the mountains. The mountain climate is mild at elevations between 3,000 and 6,000 feet (900 and 1,800 meters), with temperatures ranging between 65 and 75 degrees Fahrenheit (18 and 24 degrees Celsius). But at elevations between 6,500 and 10,000 feet (2,000 and 3,000 meters), temperatures are cool year-round. For example, Bogotá has an average temperature of 58 degrees Fahrenheit (14 degrees Celsius) in January and 57 degrees Fahrenheit (13.8 degrees Celsius) in July. Areas above 10,000 feet (3,000 meters) are colder. Elevations above 15,000 feet (4,500 meters) have permanent snow and ice cover.

Many animals live in the Andes Mountains. Eagles and the endangered Andean condor live in the mountain forests. Mountain lions prey on the agouti, paca, and capybara. Tapirs, relatives of the rhinoceros, make their homes here. The spectacled bear lives in forests. This bear species is the only one found in South America.

▼ Bogotá lies on a plateau in the Andes Mountains.

The Eastern Plains

A hot, flat region known as the Eastern Plains, or llanos, lies east of the Andes Mountains. Llanos means "plains" in Spanish. The llanos cover nearly one-third of Colombia. But only 2 percent of Colombia's people live in the Eastern Plains and Amazon Rain Forest regions. The city of Villavicencio is the largest city in the Eastern Plains region. Villavicencio is located at the foot of the Cordillera Oriental, only about 70 miles (110 kilometers) from Bogotá. Farmers use the plains' grasses to feed their cattle.

The Eastern Plains have some of the country's hottest temperatures. The average yearly temperature is above 74 degrees Fahrenheit (23 degrees Celsius). The Plains region receives an annual rainfall of 40 to 70 inches (102 to 178 centimeters), with a wet season between May and October and a dry season from November to April.

Large tributaries of the Orinoco River, including the Meta, Guaviare, and Vichada, cross the plains. These rivers carry sediment from the sandy, flat plains to the delta of the Orinoco in Venezuela. Rivers and ponds throughout the plains are home to capybaras and crocodiles. Jaguars, the largest wild cats in the Americas, prowl the llanos.

▲ Farmers use the llanos to graze cattle.

Amazon Rain Forest

The giant Amazon Rain Forest stretches north from Brazil into southern Colombia, covering the area with lush vegetation. The rain forest receives more than 100 inches (250 centimeters) of rain each year.

The Amazon River flows through the rain forest. Many tributaries of the Amazon River start in Colombia. The Putumayo River begins near the town of Pasto and forms much of Colombia's border with Ecuador and Peru.

Amazon Forest tribes occupy this region. These native peoples plant crops, fish, and hunt in the forest. The port city of Leticia lies on the Amazon River at the southern tip of Colombia. People can reach this small city of about 70,000 people by air or a long journey by boat and bus.

The Amazon Rain Forest is home to more species of animals than anywhere else on Earth. Butterflies and other insects fly throughout the rain forest. Jungle birds such as quetzals, parrots, macaws, and toucans nest among the trees. Sloths and primates such as spider and howler monkeys dangle from the branches of the tropical trees.

Jaguars

The endangered jaguar is the largest wild cat of North and South America. Jaguars can be 5 to 8 feet (1.5 to 2.4 meters) long, with a 1- to 2-foot (30- to 61-centimeter) tail. They weigh between 150 and 300 pounds (68 and 136 kilograms).

A jaguar's colorings help them blend in with the forests and plains in which they hunt. Most jaguars have brown-yellow fur covered with bordered spots. Spots on their belly and head are fully black. Melanistic jaguars are completely black from head to tail.

Jaguars hunt mainly at night, using their excellent eyesight to spot prey. Jaguars' powerful jaws can crush their prey's skull.

▲ Jaguars often rest in rain forest trees.

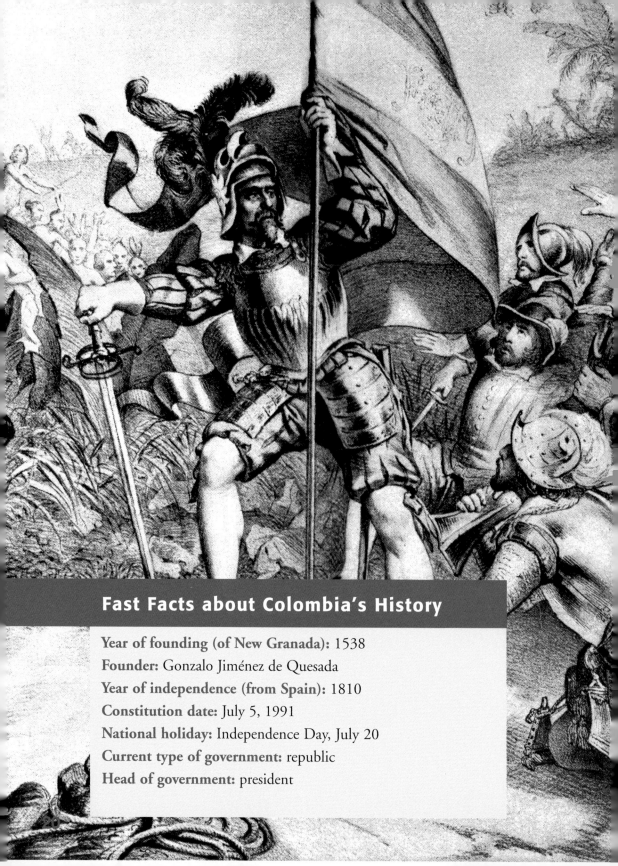

Fast Facts about Colombia's History

Year of founding (of New Granada): 1538
Founder: Gonzalo Jiménez de Quesada
Year of independence (from Spain): 1810
Constitution date: July 5, 1991
National holiday: Independence Day, July 20
Current type of government: republic
Head of government: president

Chapter 3

Colombia's History and Government

Between 12,000 and 20,000 years ago, experts believe that Asians moved across a land bridge that connected Siberia and Alaska. Many of these people, now called American Indians, moved into South America.

Most of these people hunted, fished, and farmed. The Chibcha became the largest of these tribal groups. They settled on a plateau in the Andes Mountains. The Chibcha built small wooden homes and developed a trade system with other tribes.

Spanish Conquest and Colonial Rule

Spanish explorer Alonso de Ojeda landed on Guajira Peninsula in 1499. Many Spanish expeditions followed. The search for gold drew many explorers to the new land. They founded Colombia's oldest town, Santa Marta, in 1525.

◀ Spanish explorer Alonso de Ojeda, shown here leading his men, landed in Colombia in 1499.

▶ Gonzalo Jiménez de Quesada founded Bogotá, shown here in the 1880s, on Chibcha lands.

SANTA FE DE BOGOT

In 1536, Gonzalo Jiménez de Quesada led an expedition into the Andes to the Chibcha lands. In 1538, Jiménez de Quesada conquered the Chibcha people. He founded Santafé de Bogotá on Chibcha lands. He named the area the New Kingdom of Granada, after his home region of Granada in Spain.

Spanish colonists founded many towns throughout New Granada. In 1549, the king of Spain placed New Granada under the Viceroyalty of Peru. He also established a council called the Audiencia of Santafé de Bogotá to locally manage New Granada.

American Indians who worked for the Spanish were treated harshly. They mined valuable emeralds, platinum, gold, and salt for the colonists. They also worked on farms to raise cattle, grain, and other crops. Many American Indians died of European diseases, such as smallpox, brought by the colonists. The colonists then brought slaves from Africa to work on their plantations.

> **Did you know...?**
> The people of Cartagena built a wall 39 feet (12 meters) high and 56 feet (17 meters) thick around the city to protect it from gold-seeking pirates.

Mining and farming with forced labor continued this way for more than 100 years. In 1717 and again in 1739, Spain combined the New Kingdom of Granada with the territories that are now the countries of Venezuela, Ecuador, and Panama. This large colony, with Bogotá as capital, was called the Viceroyalty of New Granada.

The Struggle for Independence

In the late 1700s, many colonists grew unhappy with Spanish rule. Spain had placed new taxes on the colonies. Creoles, Colombian-born Spaniards, were unhappy because they could not hold high positions in government reserved for native Spaniards. Many Creoles also were traders and merchants who were unhappy that the colony could not trade with any country but Spain. In 1780, they started a revolt called the Comunero Rebellion. This revolt ended in

1781 in a settlement with Spain, although a small group continued to fight.

In 1808, French emperor Napoleon Bonaparte and his army invaded Spain. Spain's South American colonies took advantage of this time to establish their independence. But people in New Granada disagreed about how they should be governed. Civil war broke out. After Napoleon's defeat in 1814, Spain sent troops to South America to reconquer its colonies. The civil war made conquest easy for Spain. People who were disloyal to Spain were killed.

Some people, like Francisco de Paula Santander, escaped and joined forces with Simón Bolívar. This Venezuelan general became known as "The Liberator." In 1819, Bolívar started a march across the plains toward Bogotá. On August 7, 1819, Bolívar's army defeated Spain in the Battle of Boyacá. Colombia won its independence. Bolívar's army obtained freedom for Ecuador and Venezuela soon after.

In 1821, colonists created a new country from present-day Venezuela, Colombia, Panama, and Ecuador. They named it Gran Colombia after Christopher Columbus. Bolívar became the first president of Gran Colombia. But by 1830, Venezuela and Ecuador had become separate nations. Colombia became known as the Republic of New Granada. Bolívar died in 1830.

▶ Simón Bolívar led the fight to free Colombia from Spain.

Political Conflict

As an independent country, Colombia was troubled by weak governments and violent conflicts. Two political parties formed—the Conservative Party and the Liberal Party. The Conservatives supported a strong Roman Catholic Church and a strong central government. The Liberals wanted to limit the power of the church and central government.

During the next 60 years, government power switched back and forth between the two parties. The parties often wrote new constitutions when they obtained power. In 1853, the Liberal Party wrote a new constitution that abolished slavery and gave more power to the states. Conservatives came to power in 1886. They wrote a constitution that established the Republic of Colombia and called for a strong central government. Liberals and Conservatives then began the War of a Thousand Days (1899–1903). Historians estimate that between 60,000 and 130,000 people died during this war.

Political conflict was not limited to Liberals and Conservatives. In 1903, the United States wanted to build a canal across the narrow isthmus connecting Colombia and Colombia's Panama territory. The people in the Panama territory wanted the canal built. With U.S. support, people in the Panama territory revolted against the Colombian government and gained independence. The United States then built the Panama Canal, which opened in 1914. The United States later paid Colombia $25 million for its loss of Panama.

In the late 1940s, disagreements between the Liberals and Conservatives again turned violent. During the presidential election of 1946, three candidates vied for the position—two Liberals and one Conservative. The two Liberal candidates split the

▼ Rioters bombed this house during La Violencia.

Liberal votes, which allowed the Conservative to have the most overall votes. The Conservative then replaced many government officials with Conservatives. The Liberals became angry about these events and the two sides began to fight. The period between 1946 and 1964 is known as "La Violencia," which means "The Violence." About 200,000 people died as a result of fighting during La Violencia.

In 1957, the Liberals and Conservatives agreed to serve alternate presidential terms and to split government positions evenly between the two parties. This agreement, called the National Front, lasted from 1958 to 1974. The new government concentrated on social and economic reform.

Guerrilla Groups

People had formed rebel guerrilla groups during La Violencia. At first, violence decreased when the National Front came to power. But some Colombians did not think the National Front was working any better than previous governments. These guerrilla groups increased in power and number after the National Front came to power. These groups believe that the government takes advantage of working-class Colombians. They are willing to use violence to bring about change.

Of these guerrilla groups, three became the most powerful. The National Liberation Army, or Ejercito de Liberación Nacional (ELN), formed in 1964. ELN members have Marxist beliefs. They feel that all property and goods belong to a community. The Colombian Revolutionary Armed Forces, or Fuerzas Armadas Revolucionarias de Colombia (FARC), formed in 1966. This group believes that Colombia should be a communist country. Communism is a way of organizing

▲ Members of FARC stand guard at peace
talks between FARC leader Manuel
Marulanda and Colombian President
Andrés Pastrana in 2000.

a country so that all land, houses, and factories are run
by the government in the interests of the community.

In 1974, a third guerrilla group formed called the
19th of April Movement, or Movimiento 19 de Abril
(M-19). They believed the presidential election of 1974
on April 19th was rigged against their candidate. The
M-19 also believed that workers and poor people
deserved better treatment. The M-19 had more support
from people in the cities than the FARC or ELN.

Drug Trafficking

While guerrilla groups were forming, people began to grow large amounts of illegal plants such as marijuana and coca. The leaves of the coca plant are used to make the drug cocaine. Loosely organized groups involved in the drug trade, called cartels, formed. Colombia became the largest producer of cocaine in the world because of its weak government and its good climate for coca crops.

The Colombian government has had a difficult time controlling the growth of coca. People make more money growing coca and marijuana crops than growing legal crops. People grow coca in the middle of jungles and on mountain slopes. Although the government is successful in destroying some coca fields, growers often start raising coca again on new sites.

Drug cartels are very rich and powerful. Cartels may control entire villages because of the jobs they provide picking coca and processing cocaine. Cartel members have killed many government officials and citizens who speak out against the drug trade.

Colombia Today

Even after the National Front agreement ended in the 1970s, Liberals and Conservatives continued to work together. But Colombians wanted a new constitution. They elected representatives, some of them from M-19,

▼ Colombians who are unhappy with government policies often protest.

to create a new constitution. This special assembly developed Colombia's ninth constitution. This constitution went into effect July 5, 1991.

Colombia faces ongoing social and economic problems. Many people live in poverty while a small number of Colombians control the country's wealth and government. This inequality leads people to protest against the government.

◀ Colombian army soldiers seize cocaine in Puerto Asis.

Guerrilla groups and drug cartels still cause problems. Colombia did come to a peace agreement with M-19 in 1990, but has not reached a settlement with the others. In 2000, Colombia instituted an aggressive drug policy that it hopes will rid the country of drugs within five years.

Colombia's Government

Colombia has been a republic with an elected government throughout most of its history. Today, all Colombian citizens 18 years of age and older can vote. The national government is composed of the executive, legislative, and judicial branches.

The president is the head of the executive branch and head of the government. The president makes decisions about new government laws and policies with the help of a group of advisers called a cabinet. The president serves a four-year term that may not be immediately repeated.

Colombia's legislative branch, called Congress, makes the country's laws. Congress consists of the Senate and the House of Representatives. Senators hold 102 seats. Representatives hold 165 seats. Both senators and representatives are elected to four-year terms.

The Supreme Court of Justice heads Colombia's judicial branch. Supreme Court judges serve one eight-year term. The Constitutional Court specifically protects the constitution and ensures that all levels of the government obey it. States also have courts.

Colombia is divided into 32 departments and the capital district around Bogotá. These departments are similar to states or provinces. Each department has an elected governor and assembly. Within departments, each city has an elected mayor and council.

Fast Facts about Colombia's Economy

System of weights and measures: metric

Major types of industry: textiles, food processing, oil, cement

Major natural resources/minerals: petroleum, natural gas, coal, iron ore, nickel, gold, copper, emeralds

Major agricultural products: coffee, bananas, rice, tobacco, corn

Major types of manufactured products: textiles, processed foods, chemicals, pharmaceuticals, metal products

Imports: industrial and transportation equipment, chemicals

Exports: coffee, petroleum, coal, salt, bananas, flowers

Chapter 4

Colombia's Economy

Colombia has one of the healthiest economies in South America. Colombia's strength in the agriculture industry is becoming balanced with its growth in the manufacturing and mining industries.

Colombia has a workforce of nearly 17 million people. Almost half of these workers are employed in the service industry. They work in banks, hospitals, schools, and government. Agriculture employs another 30 percent of Colombia's workforce. The remaining workers hold manufacturing jobs.

Agriculture and Forestry

Colombians produce a variety of agricultural products on plantations, ranches, and small farms. Colombia's largest crop is coffee, which grows in the Andes Mountains. Colombia is the second largest coffee producer in the world, behind Brazil. It produces

◀ Farmers grow coffee and other crops in the Andes Mountains.

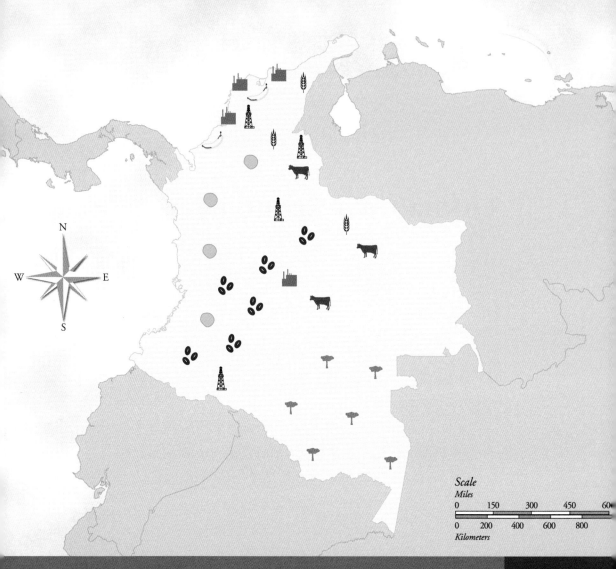

Colombia's Industries and Natural Resources

KEY

 Bananas

🫘 Coffee

🌳 Forest products

🟡 Gold

🌾 Grains

🐄 Livestock

🏭 Manufacturing

🛢 Petroleum

one-eighth of the world's coffee. Most coffee farms are small, averaging fewer than 15 acres (6 hectares) of land.

Farmers produce a variety of other crops. Bananas are Colombia's second most important crop. People grow bananas, along with cotton and sugarcane, on plantations throughout the Caribbean Coast region. Other major crops include cassava, wheat, barley, and corn. Farmers grow rice in the lowlands and potatoes in the cooler highlands. Tobacco, sesame, peanuts, and soybeans are other Colombian crops. Farmers also grow African oil palms, cacao for chocolate, grapes, citrus fruits, and cut flowers. Southern Colombians harvest lumber and rubber from the rain forest.

Colombians also raise livestock. Cattle ranches stretch across the Lowlands to the Andes Mountains and through the Eastern Plains. Ranchers also raise sheep and poultry.

Colombia is known for illegal crop production. Marijuana thrives in Colombia's fertile northeastern mountain areas. Coca is grown in isolated portions of the Amazon River basin. Many Colombian farmers find great profits and an eager market for these crops.

Manufacturing

Colombia's manufacturing industries are growing. Bogotá, Medellín, and Cali have many factories. The Caribbean coastal cities of Barranquilla and Cartagena also form an industrial base. The textile industry employs more workers than any other manufacturing industry. Many of these factories are small plants that meet the country's own needs. Larger companies manufacture textiles such as fabric and yarn for export.

Food and beverage processing and chemical production are other leading Colombian industries. Factories also produce medicines, metal products, and cement.

Mining and Energy Production

Mining industries provide about 40 percent of Colombia's foreign trade. Colombia has large coal and petroleum deposits. Most of Colombia's coal is mined in the Andes Mountains. Guajira Peninsula also contains coal deposits. Petroleum has been a major Colombian resource and export since the early 1900s. People discovered large deposits in the plains during the 1980s and 1990s. By the end of the 1990s, the country's oil production reached nearly 800,000 barrels a day.

Though plentiful, oil and coal are used for a small amount of the nation's energy needs. Hydroelectric

▲ Companies have built many pipelines
to tap into Colombia's oil reserves.

plants on Colombia's rivers produce nearly 75 percent of Colombia's electrical power.

During the colonial period, the gold industry was vital to Colombia's economy. Colombia still is a leading producer of gold, but other minerals and metals also are important. Miners collect metals such as silver, nickel, iron ore, and copper. The country also contains rich deposits of zinc, marble, limestone, sulfur, clay, mica, and talcum. Large underground salt deposits contribute to Colombia's growing chemical industry. Colombia also produces 95 percent of the world's emeralds.

Tourism

Tourists to Colombia have access to a variety of activities. Visitors to the Caribbean Sea coast can canoe in the calm ocean waters, watch whales, and snorkel among the coral reefs. People can visit one of Colombia's 33 national parks and reserves, or take a trip down the Amazon River. Colombia's art and history museums offer visitors a chance to see Colombian culture.

Colombia's history of violence hurts its tourism industry. The U.S. State Department warns U.S. citizens that they have a greater risk of being kidnapped in Colombia than in any other country in the world. Drugs, guerrilla activity, and corrupt police all hurt Colombia's reputation.

500 peso coin (front)

500 peso coin (back)

Colombia's Money

Currency exchange rates change every day. Colombia's currency is the peso. One Colombian peso equals 100 centavos. In the early 2000s, 2,243 Colombian pesos equaled 1 U.S. dollar. 1,432 Colombian pesos equaled 1 Canadian dollar.

200 peso coin

20,000 peso bill

50,000 peso bill (front)

1,000 peso coin

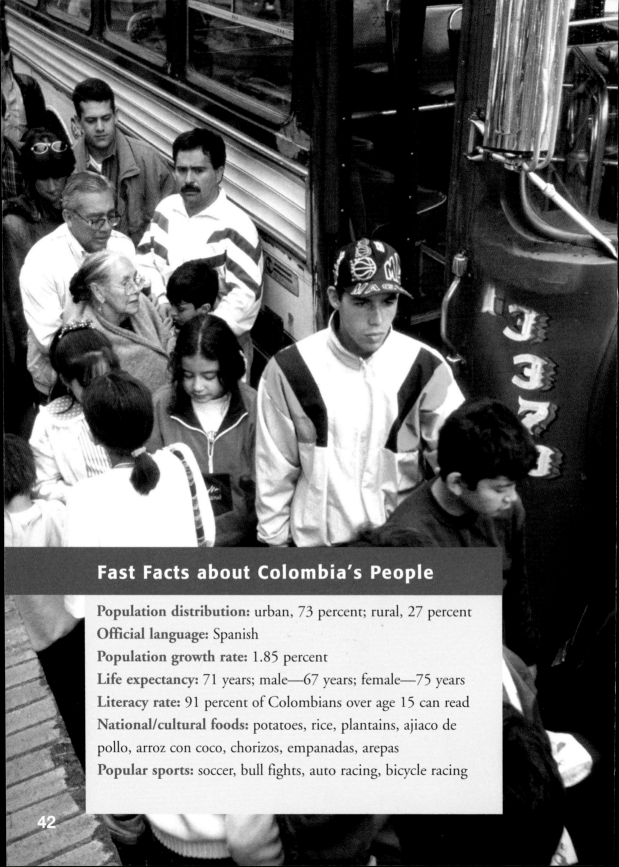

Fast Facts about Colombia's People

Population distribution: urban, 73 percent; rural, 27 percent
Official language: Spanish
Population growth rate: 1.85 percent
Life expectancy: 71 years; male—67 years; female—75 years
Literacy rate: 91 percent of Colombians over age 15 can read
National/cultural foods: potatoes, rice, plantains, ajiaco de pollo, arroz con coco, chorizos, empanadas, arepas
Popular sports: soccer, bull fights, auto racing, bicycle racing

Chapter 5

People, Culture, and Daily Life

Colombia's population is diverse. Colombians belong to several ethnic groups, yet they share similar attitudes toward religion and family. But economic class distinctly divides the population.

Ethnic Groups and Economic Classes

Ethnic groups have emerged from the American Indians, Europeans (mainly Spaniards), and Africans in Colombia. Over the years, members of these groups intermarried.

Today, mixed races account for 75 percent of Colombia's population. People with American Indian and European ancestors make up 58 percent of all Colombians. People with African and European ancestors make up 14 percent of the population. People with American Indian and African ancestors make up about 3 percent of the population.

◄ Seventy-five percent of Colombia's people have mixed-race backgrounds.

The other 25 percent of the people are of unmixed ancestry. Twenty percent are European, 4 percent are African American, and 1 percent is American Indian.

In some ways, the Colombian economic classes reflect colonial days. The small Colombian upper class is made up largely of people with European ancestors. These people tend to earn more money and be better educated than any other group. They control most of Colombia's wealth, businesses, and land. American Indians and African Americans usually hold jobs as laborers who work for the upper class.

Most of the original languages spoken by the native peoples have disappeared. Spanish, spoken by nearly the whole population, is Colombia's official language. Colombians speak a very pure form of the Spanish language and even have laws to keep it from changing.

Urban and Rural Life

Between 1938 and 1973, large numbers of Colombians moved from rural to urban areas. Many of these people wanted better lives than they had in their rural homes. Today, about 73 percent of Colombia's people live in cities. Urban dwellers have easier access to education, medical care, and modern conveniences, such as plumbing. But many also lack the education and skills needed for city jobs.

In Colombia, housing often depends on a person's income level. Some urban professional Colombians live in comfortable houses or apartments in middle-class neighborhoods. Many working-class Colombians live in shabby buildings and run-down neighborhoods. Still other urban Colombians live in worse conditions. Many newcomers from rural areas build shacks out of tin or cardboard at the edges of Colombia's large cities. These crowded settlements, called tugurios, usually

▲ This woman and her children wash clothes in the street in a Bogotá tugurio.

have no running water, electricity, or sewers. Many children in these areas become homeless "gamines," because their parents cannot support them.

Class also separates people in rural areas. A small percentage of wealthy people own much of the farmland. They hire workers to farm their land, or they rent very small areas to tenant farmers. Farm workers and tenant farmers barely produce enough to feed their families. They live in simple houses made from local materials. For example, houses in mountain regions are made with clay, also called adobe, walls. Houses in warm, wet coastal regions are made of bamboo poles and palm leaves.

Family and Religion

Colombians usually have strong family ties. Several generations may live together or nearby as neighbors. The Colombian woman's role in the family and society has gradually changed. In the past, women stayed home to care for the family while men held a job. Women were not allowed to go to school. Women in rural areas were expected to care for the home as well as do farm work or other jobs to help support the family. Women today, especially those in the upper class, still have less freedom and rights than men do.

But women of all classes are breaking out of their traditional family role, getting an education, and joining Colombia's workforce.

Roman Catholicism is Colombia's official religion. Ninety-five percent of Colombians are Catholic. Catholicism has a strong influence on Colombian society and attitudes. Catholicism influences government policies, but the Colombian constitution guarantees freedom of religion. Some small Protestant and Jewish communities exist in Colombia. Some American Indians practice their traditional religions.

Education

The Colombian government provides free public schools for children. Private schools that charge tuition to attend also are available. All children are required to attend at least five years of primary school. Those who complete primary school may move on to secondary school and higher education.

The level and quality of education depends on the area. In general, rural children receive a poorer education than urban children do. A rural school may only be able to offer two or three grades because it lacks teachers, classrooms, and materials. Rural children may live in remote areas that lack reliable transportation to school. Other children may

Learn to Speak Spanish

Colombians speak the purest form of the Spanish language in Latin America. The government has made laws to protect the language from changes.

Helpful Words:

hello—hola (OH-lah)

good morning—buenos dias (BWAYN-os DEE-ahs)

good-bye—adios (ah-dee-OHS)

please—por favor (POR fah-VOHR)

thank you—gracias (GRAH-see-ahs)

no—no (NOH)

yes—si (SEE)

Do you speak English?—
    ¿Hablas Ingles?
    (ah-BLAHS in-GLAYSS)

▲ These Bogotá schoolboys will learn to read and write Spanish.

not be able to attend school because they have to help their parents with farm work.

Efforts to reach Colombia's uneducated population have been successful. Educational radio and TV broadcasts target children and adults. During the past 50 years, the number of Colombians who can read has risen from 50 to 91 percent.

Clothing and Food

Many urban Colombians dress much like people in the United States and Canada do. But region and climate may influence clothing. People wear ruanas for warmth in the cold mountain regions. These blankets have a slit in the middle for the head.

In general, the Colombian diet includes foods such as potatoes, rice, and noodles. A typical Colombian lunch begins with soup. A person then may eat rice, potatoes, or plantains. These banana-like fruits are served fried, baked, and mashed. A meal also may include salad, fried fish or meat, fried eggs, and beans.

Many Colombians enjoy stews and thick soups, especially in the Andes Mountains. A favorite soup, ajiaco de pollo, contains potatoes, chicken, corn, and cassava. Arroz con coco, or rice with coconut, is a dish enjoyed in coastal areas.

Chorizos, empanadas, and buñuelos are popular snacks eaten throughout Colombia. Chorizos are spicy sausages. Empanadas are pastries stuffed with meat

Make Fried Plantains

Colombians often eat plantains in place of potatoes, flavoring them with salt. You also can fry plantains and serve them with sugar for a dessert. Please ask an adult to help you with this recipe.

What You Need

2 green plantains
⅓ cup (75 mL) oil
salt and butter to taste

knife
frying pan
pot holder
spoon

potato masher
mixing bowl
serving bowl

What You Do

1. Peel the plantains and chop them into ¼-inch (.6-centimeter) slices.
2. Fry the plantain slices in half of the oil on medium-low heat until they are golden brown.
3. Use the pot holder to take the frying pan off the heat. Turn off stove. Put the plantains in the bowl. Mash them with the potato masher. If they are still very hard, put them in a microwave for about 1 minute.
4. Place the frying pan back on the stove on medium heat and add the rest of the oil. Put the mashed plantains in the oil and fry for 2 to 3 minutes, but do not burn.
5. Spoon the plantains into a serving bowl and add butter and salt to taste.

Makes 4 to 6 servings.

and vegetables. Buñuelos are deep-fried balls of dough made with corn flour and cheese.

Children and adults drink agua de panela, a beverage consisting of brown sugar dissolved in water. Fresh fruit juices made from guava and mango also are common. Many Colombians drink coffee throughout the day.

Sports and Pastimes

Sports such as basketball, baseball, golf, and tennis are popular in Colombia. Soccer is Colombia's most popular sport. Colombia's national team has qualified for several World Cup finals. Colombians also attend bullfights, a traditional Spanish pastime. Auto and bicycle races also are popular. The Tour of Colombia is a yearly bicycle race that covers 1,200 miles (1,931 kilometers) in 12 days.

Colombia's landscape is a natural source of relaxation and enjoyment. Sunbathers and swimmers enjoy the beaches along the Caribbean Sea. The snow-capped Andes Mountains attract skiers.

Art and Literature

Colombian art reflects both American Indian and European cultures. Colombia's earliest works of art were created hundreds of years ago by advanced

These farmers play soccer near Cali. Soccer is many Colombians' favorite sport.

American Indian civilizations. In southern Colombia, enormous stone statues of American Indian gods still stand high in the Andes Mountains. Bogotá's Gold Museum displays figurines and elegant jewelry made by skilled American Indian goldsmiths.

After Spanish colonists arrived in Colombia, European art styles began to overshadow the American Indians' artistic traditions. The native art forms were gradually forgotten. Today, some Colombian artists incorporate these traditional methods and materials into their own art.

Many Colombians enjoy reading literature, especially poetry. Many professionals such as lawyers and teachers write poetry as a pastime. Gabriel García Márquez, a Nobel Prize-winning author, writes about Colombian life.

Holidays and Celebrations

Many regions of Colombia hold fairs and fiestas. Colombians play and dance to traditional music, and wear traditional dress at these fairs. They help preserve Colombia's rich cultural history.

Colombia has many national holidays, including Colombian Independence Day and the Battle of Boyacá. Colombian Independence Day, celebrated on July 20, marks the colonists' uprising against the Spaniards. People observe this day with patriotic music. Groups of schoolchildren and the military march through the streets of their hometowns. On August 7, people honor the Battle of Boyacá, which was the 1819 victory against the Spanish forces. People also celebrate Labor Day on May 1 to honor Colombia's workers. Columbus Day on October 12 honors the country's namesake, Christopher Columbus.

▼ Colombians watch a parade during an Independence Day celebration in Bogotá.

People celebrate religious holidays such as Christmas and Easter across Colombia. One of Colombia's liveliest celebrations is Carnival. People celebrate Carnival for four days before the Lenten period of fasting before Easter. During Carnival, people in brightly colored costumes dance and celebrate in the streets.

▲ The endangered Andean condor is Colombia's unofficial national bird. It has a wingspan of up to 10 feet (3 meters) and weighs up to 26 pounds (12 kilograms).

Colombia's National Symbols

◄ Colombia's Flag

The Colombian flag, composed of three simple horizontal stripes, was adopted in 1861. The broad yellow stripe at the top represents Colombia's gold. Beneath that, a narrower blue stripe stands for the Atlantic Ocean that separates the country from Spain. The narrow red stripe at the bottom represents the blood that was shed for independence.

◄ Colombia's Coat of Arms

The Colombian coat of arms was adopted in 1834. A condor tops the coat of arms. The coat of arms also shows a pomegranate, horns of plenty, a liberty cap, and the Isthmus of Panama, which once was part of Colombia.

Other National Symbols

National anthem: Himno Nacional (Oh Glory Unfading)

National flower: orchid

National tree: wax palm

Unofficial national bird: Andean condor

Timeline

1821
The state of Gran Colombia is created.

1717
Spain creates Viceroyalty of New Granada, combining Venezuela, Ecuador, Panama, and Colombia.

1819
Simón Bolívar's army defeats Spanish forces at the Battle of Boyacá; Colombia wins its independence.

A.D. 1499
Alonso de Ojeda lands on Colombia's Caribbean coast.

1853
A new constitution abolishes slavery.

B.C.   A.D. 1500   1700   1800

18,000–10,000 B.C.
People migrate to Colombia from Asia.

1538
Gonzalo Jiménez de Quesada founds New Kingdom of Granada and Santafé de Bogotá.

1780–1781
Colonists wage Comunero Rebellion against Spanish rule.

1830
Venezuela and Ecuador break away from Gran Colombia; Colombia becomes Republic of New Granada.

1886
A new constitution establishes the Republic of Colombia.

1946–1964
Liberals and Conservatives fight during La Violencia; 200,000 people die.

1974
The National Front ends.

1991
A new constitution is adopted.

1900   **1950**   **2000**

1899–1903
Liberals and Conservatives fight the War of a Thousand Days.

1903
Panama gains independence from Colombia.

1957
Liberals and Conservatives form the National Front.

1985
Nevado del Ruiz erupts and buries the town of Armero, killing 23,000 people.

2000
Colombia adopts a new policy that aims to stop the drug trade within five years.

Words to Know

cartel (kar-TEL)—a powerful group that seeks to control an industry; drug cartels in Colombia seek to control the drug trade.

cocaine (koh-KAYN)—an illegal drug made from the coca plant

gamines (gah-MEE-nays)—children who were forced from their homes

guerrilla groups (guh-RIL-uh GROOPS)—groups that seek to radically change the government; guerrilla groups may use violence to achieve their goals.

habitat (HAB-uh-tat)—the place and natural conditions in which a plant or animal lives

isthmus (ISS-muhss)—a narrow strip of land that lies between two bodies of water and connects two larger land masses

llanos (LAH-nos)—the Spanish word for plains

plateau (pla-TOH)—an area of high, flat land

tenant farmer (TEN-uhnt FARM-ur)—a farmer who rents and lives on land that belongs to someone else

tugurio (too-GOO-ree-oh)—a crowded, poor settlement at the edge of a Colombian city that has no running water, electricity, or sewers

To Learn More

Cameron, Sara. *Out of War: True Stories from the Frontlines of the Children's Movement for Peace.* New York: Scholastic Press, 2001.

DuBois, Jill, and Leslie Jermyn. *Colombia.* Cultures of the World. New York: Marshall Cavendish, 2002.

Goodnough, David. *Simón Bolívar: South American Liberator.* Hispanic Biographies. Springfield, N.J.: Enslow Publishers, 1998.

Meister, Cari. *Amazon River.* Rivers and Lakes. Minneapolis: Abdo Publishing, 2000.

Morrison, Marion. *Colombia.* Enchantment of the World. New York: Children's Press, 1999.

Rawlins, Carol B. *The Orinoco River.* Watts Library. New York: Franklin Watts, 1999.

Useful Addresses

Embassy of Colombia in Canada

360 Albert Street, Suite 1002

Ottawa, ON K1R 7X7

Canada

Embassy of Colombia in the United States

2118 Leroy Place, NW

Washington, DC 20008

Internet Sites

CIA The World Factbook—Colombia

http://www.cia.gov/cia/publications/factbook/geos/co.html

Information from the U.S. Central Intelligence Agency

Colombia for Kids

http://www.colombiaemb.org/English/Kids/kids.html

Facts from the Colombian Embassy in the United States

Jaguar Fact Sheet

http://www.zoo.org/educate/fact_sheets/jaguar/jaguar.htm

Habits and habitat of the largest cat in the Americas

Lonely Planet World Guide: Destination Colombia

http://www.lonelyplanet.com/destinations/south_america/colombia

Travel and background information from Lonely Planet

▲ This woman trims a carnation stem in a greenhouse near Bogotá. Colombia exports cut flowers around the world. It is one of the United States' key suppliers.

Index

agriculture, 14, 16, 17, 18, 21, 23, 35, 37, 47
Amazon Rain Forest, 9, 16, 18, 19
Amazon River, 18, 37, 40
American Indians, 21, 22, 23, 43–44, 48, 52–53
Andes Mountains, 5, 9, 13–15, 21, 22, 35, 38, 50, 52, 53
animals (*see* wildlife)
art, 40, 52–54

Battle of Boyacá, 24, 54
Bogotá (*see* Santafé de Bogotá)
Bolívar, Simón, 24, 25

Caribbean Sea, 6, 9, 11, 13, 40, 52
Cartagena, 9, 11, 38, 45
Catholicism, 25, 48
Chibcha, 21, 22
Chocó, 12, 13
climate, 9, 11, 12, 14, 16, 30, 50
clothing, 50, 54
coat of arms, 57
coca, 30, 37
cocaine, 30, 32
coffee, 35, 37, 52
Colombian Revolutionary Armed Forces (*see* Fuerzas Armadas Revolucionarias de Colombia)
Comunero Rebellion, 23–24
Conservative Party, 25–28, 30
constitution, 26, 30, 31, 33, 48
Cordillera Central, 13
Cordillera Occidental, 13
Cordillera Oriental, 13, 16
Cristóbal Colón, 11

drugs, 6, 30, 32, 40

education, 44, 48–50
Ejercito de Liberación Nacional (ELN), 28, 29
ethnic groups, 43–44

executive branch, 33

family, 43, 47–48
farming (*see* agriculture)
flag, 57
food, 38, 50–52
Fuerzas Armadas Revolucionarias de Colombia (FARC), 28–29

Galeras Volcano, 5
gold, 21, 23, 40, 53
government, 6, 23, 24, 25, 26–28, 29, 30–31, 32–33, 35, 48, 49
Granada, New Kingdom of, 22–23
Gran Colombia, 24
Guajira Peninsula, 11, 21, 38
guerrilla groups, 6, 28–29, 30, 32, 40

holidays, 54–55
housing, 21, 44, 45–47

industry, 9, 11, 35, 36, 38–40
Isthmus of Panama, 6, 26

Jiménez de Quesada, Gonzalo, 22
judicial branch, 33

language, 44, 49
legislative branch, 33
Liberal Party, 25–28, 30
literature, 54

manufacturing, 35, 38
marijuana, 30, 37
mining, 14, 23, 35, 38, 40
Movimiento 19 de Abril (M-19), 29, 30, 32

National Front, 28, 30
National Liberation Army (*see* Ejercito de Liberación Nacional)
natural resources, 36
Nevado del Ruiz, 5

19th of April Movement (*see* Movimiento 19 de Abril)

Ojeda, Alonso de, 21
Orinoco River, 16

Pacific Ocean, 6, 11, 13
Panama, 6, 23, 26
Panama Canal, 26
Paula Santander, Francisco de, 24
plains, 9, 16–17, 19, 24, 37, 38
population, 6, 43–44
president, 29, 33
Puracé Volcano, 5

rainfall, 11, 12, 16, 18
rain forest, 9, 12, 18, 19, 37
rebel groups (*see* guerrilla groups)
religion (*see also* Catholicism), 43, 48, 55
Roman Catholic Church, 25, 48

Santafé de Bogotá, 5, 14–15, 16, 22, 23, 24, 33, 38, 46, 49, 53, 55
Santa Marta, 11, 21
service industry, 35
Sierra Nevada de Santa Marta, 11
Spain, 22, 23–24, 25
Spanish explorers, 21–22
sports, 52, 53

temperature, 9, 14, 16
tourism, 6, 40

Violencia, La, 27, 28

War of a Thousand Days, 26
wildlife, 11, 12–13, 14, 16, 18–19, 56
women, 47–48
workforce, 35, 48